TIME FOR KIDS

BOOK OF HOW

D1119041

ALL ABOUT SURVIVAL

TIME FOR KIDS
Managing Editor, TIME FOR KIDS: Nellie Gonzalez Cutler
Editor, Time Learning Ventures: Jonathan Rosenbloom

Book Packager: R studio T, New York
Art Direction/Design: Raúl Rodriguez and Rebecca Tachna
Writer: Curtis Slepian
Illustrator: Felipe Galindo
Photo Researcher: Elizabeth Vezzulla
Special Thanks to: Harry Chamberlain, Anne Jewell, Zane Martin, Donna Moxley Scarborough, Neil Soderstrom, Turkey Hill Dairy

DOWNTOWN
BOOKWORKS INC.
REDESIGN BY DOWNTOWN BOOKWORKS, INC.
Project Manager: Sara DiSalvo

COVER DESIGN BY SYMBOLOGY CREATIVE
Designer: Mark Wainwright

Time
HOME ENTERTAINMENT
TIME HOME ENTERTAINMENT
Publisher Jim Childs
Vice President and Associate Publisher Margot Schupf
Vice President, Finance Vandana Patel
Executive Director, Marketing Services Carol Pittard
Executive Director, Business Development Suzanne Albert
Executive Director, Marketing Susan Hettleman
Publishing Director Megan Pearlman
Associate Director of Publicity Courtney Greenhalgh
Assistant General Counsel Simone Procas
Assistant Director, Special Sales Ilene Schreider
Senior Marketing Manager, Sales Marketing Danielle Costa
Associate Production Manager Amy Mangus
Associate Prepress Manager Alex Voznesenskiy
Associate Project Manager Stephanie Braga

Editorial Director Stephen Koepp
Senior Editor Roe D'Angelo
Editors Katie McHugh Malm, Jonathan White
Copy Chief Rina Bander
Design Manager Anne-Michelle Gallero
Editorial Operations Gina Scauzillo
Editorial Assistant Courtney Mifsud

Special Thanks to: Katherine Barnet, Brad Beatson, Jeremy Biloon, Susan Chodakiewicz, Rose Cirrincione, Assu Etsubneh, Mariana Evans, Christine Font, Hillary Hirsch, David Kahn, Jean Kennedy, Kimberly Marshall, Nina Mistry, Dave Rozzelle, Matthew Ryan, Ricardo Santiago, Divyam Shrivastava, Adriana Tierno

Contents of this book previously appeared in Time For Kids Big Book of HOW.

For information on TIME For Kids magazine for the classroom or home, go to WWW.TFKCLASSROOM.COM or call 1-800-777-8600.

For subscriptions to Sports Illustrated Kids, go to www.sikids.com or call 1-800-889-6007.

Published by TIME For Kids Books
an imprint of Time Home Entertainment Inc.
1271 Avenue of the Americas
New York, New York 10020

ISBN 10: 1-61893-359-0
ISBN 13: 978-1-61893-359-1

"TIME For Kids" is a trademark of Time Inc.

We welcome your comments and suggestions about TIME For Kids Books.
Please write to us at:
TIME For Kids Books
Attention: Book Editors
PO Box 11016
Des Moines, IA 50336-1016

If you would like to order any of our hardcover Collector's Edition books, please call us at 800-327-6388. (Monday through Friday, 7:00 a.m.– 8:00 p.m. or Saturday, 7:00 a.m.– 6:00 p.m. Central Time).

1 QGT 14

Contents

HOW to Stay Safe in a Hurricane

Hurricanes are huge storms that can cause destruction to large areas. They can last more than a week, with wind speeds of 160 miles per hour or more, and can be as wide as 500 miles. Hurricanes form over water. Because of that, states along the Gulf of Mexico and the east coast of the U.S. are often the hardest hit.

The most dangerous part of a hurricane is the storm surge. A storm's powerful winds push ocean water over the shore, causing floods. Storm surges account for most of a hurricane's damage. But if your family is prepared for a hurricane, you will be safe while you sit out the storm.

FACTOID

The deadliest hurricane in U.S. history struck Galveston, Texas, in 1900, before there were instruments that could track a hurricane's path and warn people. The storm flooded the island city, killing 8,000 people.

Before the Storm

- Protect your home and property. Windows should be covered by built-in storm panels or boarded up with plywood.
- Listen to the radio or TV for information.
- Close the storm shutters. Tie down outdoor objects or bring them indoors.
- Turn off gas and electricity if told to by officials.
- Don't use the phone except for emergencies.
- Stock up on food to eat and bottled water for drinking and flushing toilets.
- Leave your home if ordered to by local authorities. Follow their instructions.
- If you live in a building with many stories, go to the lowest level—hurricane winds are stronger at higher levels.
- If you live on a coast, or in an area near water and can't escape the storm:
  - Stay indoors during the hurricane and away from windows and glass doors.
  - Close all doors inside and outside your home.
  - Stay in a small inner room, closet, or hallwa on the lowest level.
  - Lie on the floor under a table or another strong object.

Tornadoes, earthquakes, and other natural disasters don't strike often. And you may never have to escape a fire. Still, it's always important to know what to do in case of an emergency.

After the Storm

- Don't return to a home that was damaged by floodwater before local officials declare the area safe.
- Use a phone only to report life-threatening emergencies.
- Stay off the streets. There can be electrical wires on the ground, as well as weakened walls, bridges, roads, or sidewalks.
- Don't enter a home without an adult. He or she should make sure there are no loose power lines, gas leaks, or damage to the building's structure.
- Enter the home carefully and check for damage. Be careful of loose boards and slippery floors.
- Never eat food touched by floodwater.

Hurricane Season

From June to November, storms churn over the Atlantic Ocean. Sometimes they become hurricanes that hit the islands of the Caribbean and the coast of the U.S. Take a look at how wet weather, wind, and warm ocean waters whip up these powerful storms.

1. Born in West Africa
When hot, dry air from the Sahara desert meets cooler air from the Sahel region, small storms form.

2. Across the Atlantic
Some storms may gather warm ocean moisture, speeding up as they travel west. When bands of these thunderstorms form a swirling pattern, the new system is called a tropical depression.

3. The Storm Strengthens
Winds spin around the "eye" at the storm's center. It is either a tropical storm or a hurricane, depending on the wind speed.

4. After the Storm
Hurricanes weaken over land. Some storms never hit land. Instead, they turn northeast and die out over the Atlantic Ocean.

5. Other Winds Affect the Storm
Sometimes winds near a hurricane blow in the same direction. They can help the hurricane gain strength. Winds blowing in different directions or at different speeds can tear the storm apart.

FROM TFK

NORTH AMERICA
Atlantic Ocean
EUROPE
4
AFRICA
Sahara
3 Hurricane
2 Storm system
Sahel
Pacific Ocean
Nearby winds
1
SOUTH AMERICA

HOW to Stay Safe in a Storm

Lightning is nature's fireworks. This awesome force can heat the air to a temperature as high as 60,000°F. That's hotter than the surface of the sun. The heat makes the air expand and vibrate until it produces a booming thunderclap. Every thunderstorm contains lightning, but lightning can hit you even if the storm is 10 miles away and the sky above you is cloudless. That's what's known as a "bolt from the blue."

A lightning strike can cause a lot of damage. A single bolt holds up to 1 billion volts of electricity. Like fireworks, lightning should be viewed from a distance—and a safe place.

Before Thunder and Lightning Arrive

● If you see lightning and hear thunder within 30 seconds, it means the storm is within six miles of you. Seek shelter.

● If you see lightning in the upper clouds during a thunderstorm, be careful. This kind of lightning can strike many miles away from the storm. Try to get indoors.

If You're Outside

● Immediately get inside a building or hard-top automobile. If lightning strikes a car, the electricity will go harmlessly into the ground.

● Don't stand near trees or other tall objects in an open area.

● Avoid open fields, the top of a hill, or the beach. If you're in a boat, get to land right away and seek shelter.

● Don't go into a shed or other small structure in an open area like an athletic field or park.

● Don't stand next to or touch anything metal, such as a car, bicycle, or lamppost.

● If you are swimming, get out of the water immediately. Water is a good conductor of electricity.

● In an open area or anywhere else, if your hair stands up, it could mean that conditions are right for a lightning strike. Scrunch down into a ball so you make as little contact as possible with the ground. Don't lie flat on the ground.

Building a Bolt

Ever get shocked by a spark of static electricity in the winter? That spark is a mini version of a lightning bolt. Static electricity takes place when an object packed with a charge of electrons suddenly gets rid of the charge all at once. The same thing happens in a cloud during a storm.

If You're Inside

● Do not shower, bathe, or use a landline phone during a thunderstorm. A cell phone is safe to use.

● Unplug all electronics, including appliances, TVs, computers, and air conditioners. Lightning can cause power surges, which can damage equipment.

● Don't touch anything that conducts electricity and leads to the outside, such as a window frame or pipe.

● Stay indoors for at least 30 minutes after you hear the last thunderclap.

Inside the cloud, currents of air rise and fall. An updraft carries droplets of water at the bottom of the cloud to a freezing region 35,000 to 75,000 feet high. At the same time, downdrafts send ice and hail from the top of the cloud to the bottom. When the water droplets and icy particles bump each other, electrons get knocked off the rising particles and collect on the falling particles. Soon, the bottom area of the cloud has a negative charge and the top has a positive charge.

Positive and negative charges attract each other. The electric field between the top and bottom of the cloud builds up until a giant spark of electricity—a lightning bolt—shoots from one part of the cloud to the other. Lightning can also strike between two clouds. Sometimes, the electrical charge will shoot from the cloud to the ground. But almost four-fifths of all lightning strikes take place inside the clouds.

HOW to Stay Safe During an Earthquake

Shake, rattle, and roll. That's what things do during an earthquake. When Earth's crust shifts, the ground trembles and shudders. Sometimes the shaking isn't very noticeable—hanging lights can sway or a vase might tumble. But when a strong earthquake hits, houses can come apart and highways crumble.

Unlike hurricanes and many other natural disasters, earthquakes hit without warning and can come in waves. You can't know for sure if another, even stronger earthquake will strike again. If you live in an area that has earthquakes, you probably have had drills at school so you'll know how to stay safe. But here are some reminders for you to share with your family.

Prepare for an Earthquake

- Have the entire family learn what to do during an earthquake. Practice what you have learned. For some tips, go to earthquake.usgs.gov.
- Identify the safest places in each room to take cover. During family drills, practice going to those areas.
- Write down the addresses and phone numbers for where your family members are during the day, such as schools and businesses. All the members of your family should carry this list.

During an Earthquake

If you are indoors:

- Drop to the floor, take cover by getting under a strong desk or other piece of furniture, and hold on until the shaking stops. If there isn't a desk or table, cover your head with your arms and crouch down in an inside corner of the building.
- Keep away from glass, windows, outside doors and walls, and anything that can fall, such as a bookshelf or hanging light.
- If you are in bed when a quake hits, stay there. Put a pillow over your head for extra safety. If you are under something that could topple on you, move to a safer place.
- Don't leave until the shaking stops and you are certain it is safe to go outside.
- Never use an elevator during an earthquake.

If you are outdoors:

- Stay outdoors, and move away from buildings, streetlights, and electrical wires.
- Stay in the open until there is no more shaking.

An earthquake hit Haiti in 2010, killing about 200,000 people. It also caused billions of dollars of damage.

Shake but Don't Break

Architects, engineers, and scientists have made lots of progress in building structures that can withstand a quake. Buildings often collapse when they sway back and forth during an earthquake. Earthquake-proof buildings don't sit directly on the ground. They float on ball bearings, springs, or padded cylinders. During a quake, the buildings move with the wind, swaying a few feet from side to side. This keeps the structure standing.

Engineers have developed sensors to make these buildings even safer. The sensors detect shaking and "tell" the building how to move. This cuts down on how much the structure shakes.

New technology will continue to protect buildings and the people in them during a quake.

Structures that are not built to withstand earthquakes may crumble during a powerful quake. This building is in Concepción, Chile, a city that was hit by a quake in 2010.

After an Earthquake

● When the shaking stops, make sure everyone is okay.

● Adults should check the home for areas made unsafe by the earthquake.

HOW to Stay Safe in a Fire

Do you know what to do if you smell smoke in your home? Most people don't. That's the point of Fire Prevention Week, held every year in early October. During the week, firefighters teach people about fire safety.

The leading cause of home fires is cooking. If you cook, stay in the kitchen while food is on the stove. Turn off the stove if you leave the kitchen. The second biggest cause of home fires is heating. A space heater can start a fire if it is placed too close to objects that can burn. Kids can help prevent fires by not playing with matches or candles.

In case of fire, it's important that everyone in your family knows what to do to stay safe. Here are some tips:

DID YOU KNOW?

● Benjamin Franklin formed one of the first volunteer fire companies in America in 1736, in Philadelphia, Pennsylvania. He was also the first fire chief.

● Dalmatians aren't just cute black and white spotted dogs in Disney movies. They have long been the watch dogs of firehouses. The reason? Fire engines were once driven by horses. Dalmatians form a close bond with horses and would protect them from horse thieves.

Plan Ahead

● Draw a map of your home that shows the fastest way out of every room, especially the bedrooms. Babysitters should also know these paths.

● Place emergency numbers next to every phone. Save 911 or another emergency number in cell phones.

● Test all smoke alarms once a month. Make sure there is one on every level of your home. Change the batteries yearly, and replace the alarms every 10 years.

● Clear all exit routes in your house. Take things off stairs and make sure doors and windows open easily.

● Pick a meeting place outside your home where family members can gather after they leave the building if it catches on fire.

● Hold fire drills when everyone is home and hold them at different times of the day.

During a Fire

● If there is a fire, crawl or roll to the door of your room. To check if the fire is near the door, feel the doorknob with the back of your hand and the cracks around the door for heat. If the door is warm, you may have to get out another way, like through a window.

● To exit from an upper window, you need a portable escape ladder. All upper-story bedrooms should have escape ladders. Don't practice climbing down one in a drill. They should only be used in emergencies. If you don't have a ladder, hang a white or light-colored sheet out the window. That will alert firefighters that you are in the room.

● Smoke rises, so get out of the house by bending down or crawling to the exit.

● Close all doors behind you.

● Never stop to take anything with you during a fire.

● Never go back into the building if it catches on fire.

● When you're outside, call the fire department or emergency number.

Getting into Gear

Firefighters need a lot of protection when they go into a burning building. A hundred years ago, firefighters wore wool pants and shirts. Today's firefighting clothing, called turnout gear, provides better insulation. Firefighters wear several layers: one resists heat up to 1,000°F, another is water resistant, and a third is fire-resistant. The gear is so effective, firefighters sometimes don't realize how hot a fire is. New gear is solving that problem. The clothing comes with sensors that warn the firefighter when temperatures in a building are dangerously high.

All firefighters wear helmets, and early versions were made of leather and later aluminum. Nowadays, high-tech helmets are resistant to heat, flames, and electricity. They cover the ears and neck and have a shield that covers the face.

Firefighters can lose their way in the heavy smoke. GPS devices help guide them to fellow firefighters who are missing. If a firefighter passes out from the smoke, small motion devices will set off an alarm when no motion is detected. A new type of camera allows firefighters to see in dark and smoke-filled areas. The camera senses differences in temperatures, so users can detect how hot an object is or where a person is located. It can let a firefighter know if the room is ready to ignite in flames or if a floor has become weak from heat. Hot stuff!

HOW to Stay Safe During a Tornado

The United States is twister central. More tornadoes hit the U.S. than any other country. Each year, about 1,300 touch down here.

Tornadoes come in all sizes and speeds. They can spin from 86 miles per hour to 200 miles per hour or faster. Some tornadoes measure only a few feet in diameter, while some are as wide as a mile. A tornado can last a few seconds or spin for more than an hour and travel 50 miles or more. No matter how long a tornado lasts, it can threaten lives and property. A tornado will pick up cars, trees, homes, and anything else in its path. But if you know what to do when a twister hits, you can stay safe.

FACTOID

Most twisters in the U.S. touch down in Tornado Alley. That's the nickname given to the states in the central United States. But twisters have struck every state at one time or other.

Before a Tornado Hits

● Make sure your family has a plan in place for when you are at home, at school, or outdoors.

● Hold drills so you know what to do in case a tornado approaches.

● The National Weather Service broadcasts warnings and forecasts. Know what these expressions mean:

• Tornado Watch: Stay alert for approaching storms.

• Tornado Warning: Go to a safe place.

• Severe Thunderstorm Warning: Tornadoes can form in areas hit by powerful thunderstorms.

● Check the skies for storms that are coming your way. Look for these danger signs:

• The wind dies down suddenly, and the air becomes very still

• Large, dark, low-lying clouds

• A cloud of debris in the sky

• A loud roar that sounds like a train coming in your direction

● If you see any signs of a possible tornado, take shelter right away.

Tornadoes usually form during giant thunderstorms called supercells. Fast-moving winds above and slow-moving winds below set a horizontal tube of air spinning. Rising warm air tilts the tube until it is vertical. Cooler air pulls the tube to the ground. A tornado is formed. Many tornadoes are brown or black from the dust and dirt they suck up through the vortex, or center.

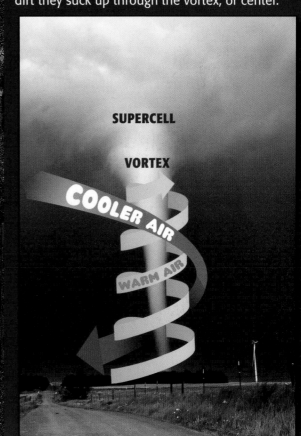

SUPERCELL

VORTEX

COOLER AIR

WARM AIR

During a Tornado

If you are indoors:

● Go to a sheltered area, such as a basement, storm cellar, or an inner room of a building's lowest level.

● Stay away from corners, windows, and doors. Move as far away as possible from the outside walls.

● Go under a heavy table and protect your head and neck with your arms.

● Do not open any windows.

If you are outdoors:

● Lie down in a ditch or low area and stay as flat as possible. Cover your head with your hands.

● Do not go under an overpass or bridge.

● If you are in a car or truck, leave the vehicle for shelter. Don't try to outrun a tornado.

● Watch out for flying objects.

A researcher sets up equipment to gather information about a fast-approaching twister.

HOW Does a Search Dog Find a Missing Person?

You've probably heard the old saying that dogs are a human's best friend. For members of a police force, search and rescue dogs are the best of the best. Search and rescue (SAR) canines are used to find people lost in the woods or buried under the rubble of collapsed buildings. SAR dogs are specially trained to detect human scent. They've found people buried 20 feet under snow. The reason: a dog's nose is 10,000 times more sensitive than a human's.

SAR dogs go anywhere to help find people. These daring, brave canines are really top dogs!

Trailing and Tracking Dogs

These dogs search for a particular person. The dog is given an object that has the person's scent, such as a comb or piece of clothing. Then, the dog sniffs out that particular scent on the ground. The scent can stick to grass, branches, and other objects.

Air-scent Dogs

These dogs are trained to pick up the scent of a human. People give off millions of tiny particles, including skin cells, bacteria, and sweat. Dogs can detect these particles in the air and on the ground. Air-scent dogs, such as bloodhounds, roam free in large areas to find a human scent and lead their handler to the source.

FACTOID

SAR dogs must be trainable, able to get in and out of tight spots, have great energy, and get along with people and other dogs. They are usually large breeds, such as German shepherds, Dobermans, rottweilers, golden retrievers, giant schnauzers, or Labradors.

Avalanche Dogs

Some SAR dogs are trained to find people buried under snow. When oils on a person's skin warm up, their scent rises right up through snow. An avalanche dog can detect the scent above the surface of the snow and alert rescuers.

Disaster Dogs

They are trained to find human scent like the other SAR dogs. But they must be able to move in and around rubble from collapsed buildings and other dangerous ground. The dogs can't be afraid of splinters of wood, sharp points of steel, or broken glass. Dust and noise don't bother these incredible canines.

To the Rescue

Dogs aren't the only animals that give humans a helping hand. Here are a few other critters that serve people:

Miniature Horses They have been used as guide animals for blind people and to pull wheelchairs.

Capuchin Monkeys These monkeys can act as the hands for people in wheelchairs or who can't get around easily. The monkeys are quick learners and can help a human for 25 to 30 years. The monkeys can use their hands to turn doorknobs or the pages of a book.

Cats Cats, as well as dogs, are used as pet therapy for people in hospitals and nursing homes. Petting an animal can make people feel better and can lower their blood pressure.

HOW to Make a Compass

It's not easy to get lost. Today, people have excellent maps and a GPS satellite system to show them where they are. A thousand years ago, people didn't have either. When they were sailing on the ocean, it was tough for them to figure out their location. Around 1100 A.D., sailors came up with a way to help them navigate: a compass. Their compass was a magnetized needle that floated in a bucket of water. Today, there are many types of compasses, but the compass used by ancient sailors can still point you in the right direction.

Compass Points

Magnetic compasses work because the Earth is a giant magnet. Deep in the planet's core is a molten ball of iron. The rotation of the Earth makes the liquid iron spin, which produces a magnetic field. The north end of Earth's magnetic field is located near the North Pole. The south end is near the South Pole. A compass is a magnet with north and south ends. Since opposites attract, the south end of a magnet points toward the magnetic north. The north end points to the magnetic south.

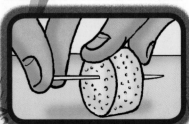

What You Need

- Sewing needle about 1 inch long
- Small bar magnet or refrigerator magnet
- Small piece of cork
- Glass or cup of water

What to Do

1 Rub the magnet against the needle in one direction for a minute or so. Make sure you move the magnet in the same direction each time.

2 Stick the needle through the center of the cork. The ends of the needle should stick out from the cork. Be careful so you don't stick yourself.

3 Put the needle and cork in the glass of water and place the glass on a table. The cork and needle should float freely, more or less parallel to the surface of the water. The glass should be wide enough so the ends of the needle don't touch the sides of the glass.

4 The needle should spin and eventually point in one direction.

5 Move the bar magnet near your compass. What happens?

Why It Happened

By rubbing the needle against the magnet, the needle became magnetized. Floating in water, the compass rotates in the direction of Earth's magnetic field. It points to either the North or South Pole, depending on which is closer to you.

Lost and Found

Even with a compass, it is possible to get lost in the woods if you're hiking. Here are some tips in case it ever happens:

⭕ Never go on a hike without an adult.

⭕ Make sure a relative or friend knows where you will be hiking.

⭕ If you are lost, stay in one place or area. Do not wander around looking for help—help will find you.

⭕ Keep warm and dry while waiting for someone to come for you. Cover up your exposed skin. Wear a hat to keep your head warm.

⭕ Stay together with the other hikers. You can hold on to each other to keep warm.

⭕ Find a comfortable place to stay that will keep you out of wind and rain. Wait under a large tree, for example, where searchers can easily see you.

⭕ Attract attention. Wear something bright to stand out. Try to make a flag out of any light-colored paper, ribbon, or other objects you have.

⭕ Do not lie down on the bare ground. The cold ground will drop your body temperature. To stay warm, cover the ground and yourself with a thick layer of branches, moss, or leaves.

⭕ Don't eat anything you find in the woods. It's better to be hungry than sick.

HOW to Make a Survival Kit

Hurricanes, floods, earthquakes, tornadoes, fires. Each year, disasters affect thousands of people. And when trouble hits, the Federal Emergency Management Agency (FEMA) comes to the rescue. The U.S. agency's job is to find places to live for people who have lost their homes due to disasters. FEMA helps repair homes and fixes public buildings that have been damaged. It provides supplies, workers, and equipment to communities that have been hit hard by nature's fury.

FEMA also trains firefighters and other emergency workers before a problem occurs so they will be ready to help out. The agency suggests that families keep a survival kit available. To the right are what FEMA says should be in the kit.

A Helping Hand

FEMA is one of many organizations that help the victims of disasters and emergencies. Here are a few others:

American Red Cross provides emergency aid, including food stations, shelter, first aid, clothing, home repairs, and medical supplies. The organization is on the scene when other relief assistance isn't enough.

Children's Disaster Response trains volunteers who help children after disasters. It works with parents, community agencies, and schools to help concerned adults understand the needs of children.

Mennonite Disaster Services provides volunteers to clean up and remove rubble from damaged homes and help repair the houses.

Friends Disaster Service helps the elderly, the disabled, and people who don't have much money or insurance after a disaster.

National Emergency Response Team helps out disaster victims by providing trailers that house 8 to 10 people.

Store at least three gallons of water per person. Buy bottled water and don't open it until you need it.

Store a supply of canned food and a nonelectric can opener. You should not have to refrigerate, cook, or add water to these foods. Choose cans that are small and light. Don't choose foods that make you thirsty. And don't forget your vitamins.

Include a first-aid kit that contains such basics as adhesive bandages, scissors, antiseptic, safety pins, soap, aspirin, and anti-bacteria cream.

Store warm clothing. There should be at least one complete change of clothes for each person, including rain gear, sturdy shoes, and gloves.

Include sanitation items, such as toilet paper, liquid detergent, a plastic bucket with a tight lid, disinfectant, toothbrushes, and toothpaste.

Also store tools such as a battery-powered radio, a flashlight, extra batteries, a fire extinguisher, paper plates and cups, and plastic storage containers.

Keep important family documents in a waterproof container, including IDs, family records, credit card numbers, and important telephone numbers.

Don't forget some fun stuff, such as games and books.

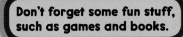

HOW Are Computers and Other Electronics Recycled?

Many people know how to recycle plastic, glass, metal, and paper products. But how do we get rid of computers, cell phones, TVs, and other electronic devices that we don't want?

What should people do with them when they want to get rid of the machines? One solution is to give away useable electronics to schools, charities, and other groups. If the device can't be reused, it can be recycled.

See how a large recycling plant takes gadgets apart and puts some back together.

Every day, recycling plants receive **electronic waste (e-waste)**, including cell phones, computers, cameras, and printers.

Workers stack **discarded computers** that will be stripped of their parts.

It's important to protect the environment. This chapter shows some ways we can reduce energy use and save our natural resources.

3

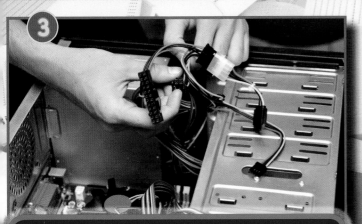

Computers are taken apart. The pieces from these and other gadgets are stored according to what they are made of. As many of the parts as possible are recycled—from plastic wrapping to broken glass and metal scraps. These are sold to separate recycling factories.

5

Much e-waste contains parts, such as circuits, that will be sold to manufacturers and used again in new products or in rebuilt devices.

4

E-waste that can't be broken apart by workers is fed into machines that separate out pieces made of different materials, such as copper. Many electronics contain small amounts of valuable metals, such as gold, which are removed and sold. Dangerous materials, such as lead, are also removed and sent to special landfills and waste plants.

DID YOU KNOW?

○ About 37,500 pounds of gold can be recovered from 500 million recycled cell phones.

○ The U.S. government has a website that lists e-waste recycling information: http://www.epa.gov/osw/conserve/materials/ecycling/donate.htm.

HOW Can You Make Your House Greener?

Going green means trying to reduce pollution and preserve natural resources. People can go green at school, at work, and especially at home. From the materials used in its construction to where the windows are placed, there are many ways to make a green building. One way is to build it with materials that don't harm the people inside or the environment. Another way is to make sure the building doesn't use a lot of energy for heating or cooling. Eco-friendly buildings are often powered by sustainable resources such as sunlight. Green builders also try to recycle and reuse materials in their buildings.

Going green can save money on energy bills and be better for the health of people—and the health of the planet. Check out some ways to help make a home more friendly to the environment.

1. Solar panels on the roof can generate electricity from sunlight.

2. Bring into the house plants that remove pollutants from the air. Two of these are English ivy and spider plants.

3. A thermostat can be programmed to keep a house cooler in the winter and warmer in the summer. This saves energy.

4. Floors and furniture can be made from reused wood, which is wood recycled from old buildings or thrown-out furniture. Use wood, such as bamboo, that doesn't come from endangered forests.

5. Use cloth towels and napkins instead of ones made from paper.

6. Use slow-flow faucets in the kitchen and bathroom. They reduce the amount of water used for washing and showering.

7. Replace regular incandescent lightbulbs with compact fluorescent bulbs to save electricity.

8. New toilets cut down on the amount of water used for each flush.

9. When computers and other electronics are turned off, they still use power. Connect them to a power strip that you can turn off to stop the drain of electricity. Or just unplug the items when not in use.

10. Plant shade trees and put up awnings or shades to keep sunlight from making the house too warm. Inside, cool off with fans instead of air conditioners.

11. To reduce energy use, insulate the walls to keep heat and cold from escaping outside.

12. Fill in the openings around doors and windows to keep out the weather.

13. All new appliances should have an ENERGY STAR label on them, especially the refrigerator, which uses a great amount of energy. Products with these labels use less electricity than older models.

HOW Do Wind Turbines Make Electricity?

Wind can sometimes be a destructive force. But wind is also a great help to humans. Over the centuries, windmills have been used to pump water, drain lakes, cut wood, and grind grain. Today, a kind of windmill is being used to produce electricity. Called wind turbines, these machines make in one year only a little more than 4% of the total electricity generated in the U.S. Still, this is enough to power 15.5 million homes.

The amount of electricity generated by wind has been growing over the last few years. One big reason is that wind is renewable energy, which means it will never run out. Also, wind turbines don't cause pollution, are cheap to run, and don't take up much space compared with the energy they produce. Some people think the answer to our energy problems is blowing in the wind.

FACTOID

The largest wind turbine blade in the world is 274 feet long.

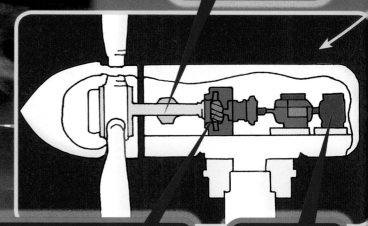

Wind makes the lightweight blades turn. The faster the blades spin, the more electricity is produced. The blades are connected to the drive shaft.

As the blades turn, the drive shaft spins. The drive shaft is connected to the gears.

The drive shaft turns gears, which make another drive shaft spin even faster. This drive shaft leads to a generator.

The generator changes the spin of the drive shaft into an electrical current.

Wind turbines are built tall to catch winds that blow high above the ground. Most are as tall as a 20-story building, while some are twice that tall.

The casing holds the drive shaft, gears, and a generator.

Ill Winds?

Not everyone loves wind power. Some people complain that the huge machines make the landscape ugly. Wind turbines also make a steady noise, which bothers some people. Some environmentalists oppose wind turbines because they believe the spinning blades sometimes kill birds and bats.

Those in favor of wind turbines say the machines help the environment. Wind turbines are a clean source of energy and will reduce the use of polluting fossil fuels, such as coal and gas. The controversy continues to swirl.

TOP 5 Wind-Power-Generating States

1. Texas
2. Iowa
3. California
4. Oklahoma
5. Illinois

Source: U.S. Energy Information Administration

Electricity from the generator flows down wires to a transformer. This device makes the current stronger. The electricity is sent through power lines to homes and towns.

FACTOID

Wind farms are large groups of wind turbines. The largest onshore wind farm in the United States is the Alta Wind Energy Center in California. Its 586 wind turbines produce enough energy to power 450,000 homes.

HOW to Make a Landfill

Every year, the average American throws away about 1,600 pounds of garbage. About 54% of all trash in the U.S. goes into landfills—large areas of land in which waste material is buried. About 12% of trash is burned in incinerators to produce energy. The rest of the trash is recycled or composted.

Landfills are designed to prevent dangerous waste from escaping into the soil and getting into the water supply. A thick layer of clay or plastic separates the garbage from the ground. Every day, workers add a layer of soil to cover the trash on top. But just because garbage is at a dump doesn't mean it disappears. Many materials don't decompose, or break down, very quickly. To see what does and doesn't decompose in a landfill, try this experiment:

What You Need

- Rubber gloves
- A large or medium-sized clay flowerpot
- A small stone
- Some soil
- Food scraps, leaves, nonglossy paper, polystyrene foam, plastic sandwich bags, aluminum foil
- Water
- 2 glass plates
- Newspapers

What to Do

1 Put the stone over the hole at the bottom of the flowerpot. This will keep water from draining out of the hole too quickly.

2 Fill one-third of the flowerpot with soil.

3 Tear up the garbage (the food scraps, leaves, and so on) into small pieces. Place the pieces on top of the soil in the flowerpot.

4 Cover the garbage with another layer of soil. The soil should just about fill the flowerpot. Pour just enough water into the flowerpot so it's completely damp, but not soaking wet.

5 Cover the top of the flowerpot with the glass plate. Put the other plate under the flowerpot so water and soil won't leak out from the bottom.

6 Put the flowerpot in a warm, dark place, such as under the kitchen sink. Check every few days. Add more water to keep the soil damp.

7 At the end of one month, take out the flowerpot and empty it on a large piece of newspaper. (Get your parents' okay first.) Put on rubber gloves and spread out the soil so you can see the condition of the garbage.

What Happened

The food, paper, and leaves should have broken down into soft material. This happens when bacteria in the soil feed on organic, or "living," materials. The plastic, foam, and foil are not organic. Bacteria can't break them down.

Air and water in the flowerpot allow bacteria to live. In a landfill, layers of soil and trash press down so tightly water and air can't get in. Bacteria can't survive, so even organic materials such as paper don't break down easily.

HOW to Make Recycled Paper

Paper was probably invented in China in 105 A.D. Before then, people wrote on anything that was handy, from cave walls and wet clay to animal skins and plants. True paper is made from tiny plant fibers, such as cotton or wood, that have been softened and pressed into thin sheets.

The U.S. uses about 69 million tons of paper and paper products each year. The good news is that about half of these products, which include money, bandages, egg cartons, and masking tape, are made from recycled paper. The more paper that's recycled, the less paper that ends up in a dump. Recycling also saves trees and the water used to make paper. So help the environment—and have fun—by making new paper from old.

What You Need

- 6 or 7 sheets of newspaper
- Glass bowl
- Cornstarch
- Hot water
- Measuring spoon
- Aluminum foil
- Wooden spoon
- Kitchen strainer
- Scissors
- Sharpened pencil
- Sponge

What to Do

1 Cut or tear four to five sheets of newspaper into the smallest pieces you can make.

2 Put the shredded paper into the bowl and cover with hot water. Mix the paper in the water with a spoon. Let it stand for several hours, stirring once in a while.

3 When the paper looks very mushy, put one or two tablespoons of cornstarch into the bowl, add more hot water, and stir again with the spoon.

pulpy paper from the strainer to the sheet of foil. Spread it out on the foil in any shape you wish your page to look like.

4 Fold a sheet of aluminum foil into the size of the sheet of paper you want to make. Poke several dozen small holes in the foil with the sharpened pencil. Put it aside for later use.

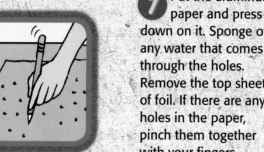

7 Put the aluminum foil with holes on top of the paper and press down on it. Sponge off any water that comes through the holes. Remove the top sheet of foil. If there are any holes in the paper, pinch them together with your fingers.

5 Using a spoon or ladle, transfer the softened paper from the bowl into the strainer and let the water drain.

8 Place another sheet of foil on top of the paper. Put a book as large as the paper on top of the foil and press down to flatten the paper. Remove the book and top foil and let the paper dry overnight. When the paper is dry, carefully peel it off the bottom sheet of foil. You can leave the edges of the paper rough or trim them with scissors. Grab a pen and see if you have the write stuff!

6 Tear off another sheet of aluminum foil that's a little larger than the size of the page you want to make. Place the foil on the remaining sheets of newspaper. With a spoon, transfer the

HOW Does a Microwave Oven Cook Food?

There's fast food. And then there's faster food. A microwave oven can heat up some foods in a minute or less.

A microwave oven cooks with a type of radiation called microwaves, which are similar to the waves that transmit TV. Microwaves don't heat air. Instead, they penetrate food, making the food's water and fat molecules vibrate. The vibrations produce heat in a jiffy. Microwaves don't heat up plastic, ceramics, paper, or glass. So, food in a microwave often sits on plates made of these materials. When you pull out a cool plate from a microwave, it can fool you into thinking the food isn't hot. But it is—so be careful before you take a bite!

Microwaves cause water to vibrate in the food more than 2 billion times a second. This vibration causes friction, which produces energy in the form of heat. Foods won't cook unless they are in— or contain—some water.

A turntable spins so the microwaves reach all parts of the food.

Microwaves bounce off a kind of fan called a stirrer. This scatters the microwaves throughout the oven. The microwaves bounce around until they enter the food.

Electricity passes through a tube called a **magnetron**, which produces microwaves. This energy is aimed at the stirrer.

Microwave Man!

Percy Spencer is the father of fast food. In 1946, Spencer was testing a device called a **magnetron** in a lab when he discovered something strange. A candy bar in his pocket had melted. Spencer put some unpopped popcorn near the magnetron. Pretty soon, the popcorn started popping. Spencer realized that microwaves produced by the magnetron could cook food. Spencer and the company he worked for eventually built a

microwave oven. It was more than five feet high and two feet wide and weighed 670 pounds. The huge oven was used in commercial kitchens. It wasn't until about 20 years later that a smaller, home version of the microwave oven was introduced. It soon became a popular cooking tool in people's kitchens.

FACTOID

Microwaves can penetrate pizza, but not the door of a microwave oven. The door is covered by a metal mesh that blocks the microwaves. The holes in the mesh are big enough to see through but too small for microwaves to pass through.

HOW Does a Lock Work?

There are locks for bikes, locks for bank vaults, locks for doors and windows, locks for diaries, and locks for lockers. Just about everyone keeps valuables under lock and key. And people have been doing that since the time of the ancient Egyptians, who made large wooden locks and keys about 4,000 years ago. The ancient Romans and Chinese weren't very trusting either. They built simple locks from metal.

Locks didn't change much until the end of the 1700s, when a few Englishmen began to make more secure devices. Today, a variety of locks keep items safe, from combination locks with numbered dials to vaults that use timing devices to locks that operate with magnetic keys.

One of the most common locks used today is a cylinder with pins inside. To open it, the pins are lifted by a key with the right shape. This is called a pin and tumbler lock.

A Pin and Tumbler Lock

1

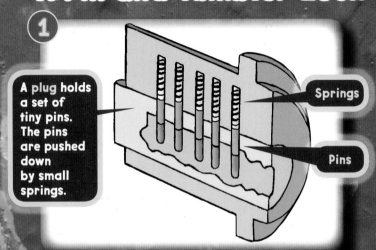

A plug holds a set of tiny pins. The pins are pushed down by small springs.

Springs

Pins

2

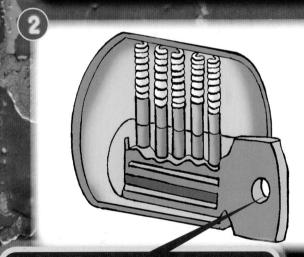

The pins prevent the plug from turning. The key slides into the plug. If the key has edges with the correct shape, it will push up the pins until they are out of the way.

3

Lock and Roll

Not many locks could hold **Harry Houdini**, who lived from 1874 to 1926. The world's most famous escape artist, Houdini would let himself be locked up in ways that seemed impossible to get out of. Yet he always escaped. In the early 1900s, Houdini challenged police in many cities to chain and handcuff him and lock him in the local jail cell. Each time, Houdini escaped. He also escaped from many hair-raising situations, such as a locked crate thrown into a river and a locked glass container filled with water.

How did he do it? Houdini knew how to pick, or "open," just about any type of lock. He was able to open handcuffs by banging them against something hard. He knew how to open a lock with a shoestring. Houdini also cheated: He hid tools for opening locks, as well as keys. When he couldn't hide a key, he swallowed it and brought it up when no one was looking. If his hands were bound, he could turn the key with his teeth!

Now the key can turn the plug. A key with the wrong-shaped edges won't lift all the pins out of the way, and the key won't turn.

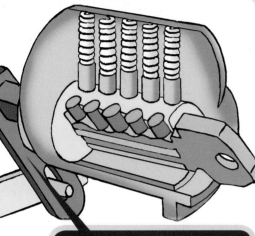

The cam is attached to the bolt, which extends into the door. When the plug turns, the cam turns as well, pulling the bolt.

When the bolt is pulled by the cam, that unlocks the door.

FACTOID

In 1844, Linus Yale Sr. invented a pin tumbler lock that fit in a cylinder. His son Linus Jr. improved the lock, which today is called a Yale lock.

HOW Does a Zipper Zip?

How could we live without zippers? Well, people managed to survive without them for thousands of years. In ancient times, people held together their animal-hide clothes with pins made of thorns. Later civilizations, such as the Greeks and Egyptians, kept clothes from opening with metal pins, clasps, or cloth ties. A major fastener advance came in the Middle Ages with the invention of the button (and the buttonhole, of course). In the 1800s, two more improvements were introduced: safety pins and snaps.

The big fastener breakthrough came from Gideon Sundback. He invented the modern zipper in 1913. Still, this fastener didn't catch on until the 1923, when it got the name *zipper*. Suddenly, zippers were sewn into just about anything that opened and closed, from dresses to rubber boots. Is the zipper an important invention? Look in your closet: It's an open and shut case!

FACTOID

The word *zipper* is an example of onomatopoeia (on-oh-*mah*-toh-pee-ah). This means giving a word a name that imitates the sound the word is associated with. *Zipper* sounds like the noise a zipper makes. A few other such words are splat, buzz, snort, honk, tinkle, beep, crash, sizzle, slurp, and whir. Can you think of other examples of onomatopoeia?

A pull tab moves the slider up and down.

Each track holds a row of teeth. The teeth on one track mesh with those on the other track.

A zipper has two tracks.

On one side of each tooth is a bump called a **hook**. The hooks of one track of teeth lock into the hollows of the other track of teeth.

On the other side of each tooth is a small dimple called a **hollow**.

The **slider** opens and closes the zipper. Inside the slider are little wedges. When zipping closed, the wedges lock the hooks into the hollows. When zipping open, the wedges pop the hooks off the hollows.

Fasten-ating Invention

Instead of zippers, some clothes and other items are fastened with Velcro, which is the brainchild of Swiss engineer Georges de Mestral. In 1941, after taking his dogs out for a walk in the woods, he noticed burrs sticking to the animals' fur. De Mestral thought those clingy seed pods from the **burdock plant** might have a use.

After eight years of testing, he invented a fastener based on the burr. It came in two parts: a cotton strip covered with tiny hooks that stuck to another cotton strip covered with tiny loops. He called his invention Velcro, a combination of the words *velvet* and *crochet* (croh-shay). (Crochet is a kind of knitting.) Later, nylon replaced cotton, and Velcro became the new zipper.

Today this hook and loop fastener is used on everything from hospital gowns, airplane seat cushions, and diapers to car floor mats, carpets, and blood pressure cuffs that go around your arm. NASA attaches Velcro to objects to keep them from floating around in space. Velcro is a perfect invention except for one thing...that ripping sound!

HOW Does a Refrigerator Keep Food Cold?

Food needs to chill out. When the temperature is above 40°F, bacteria can grow in food and spoil it. Refrigerators cool things down so food won't go bad. What did people do before there were fridges like the ones we have? They packed food in snow and ice, put it underwater, or placed it in cool cellars.

Today, cooling is more complicated. Inside a refrigerator are pipes filled with a fluid called a refrigerant. As this chemical passes through the pipes, it changes from a liquid to a gas and back to a liquid, over and over. As the liquid refrigerant circulates through the inside of the fridge, heat makes the liquid evaporate, or "turn into gas." As the gas absorbs more and more heat, everything in the fridge—including food—gets cold. This happens when you sweat on a warm day. As the sweat evaporates, your skin chills. Cool!

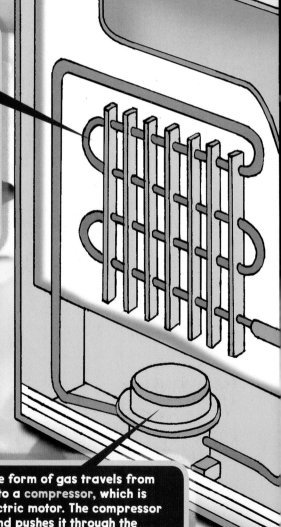

2. The compressor sends the hot gas through condensers, which are coils of tubes outside the fridge. The outside air cools the gas. As it cools, the gas condenses, turning into a liquid.

1. Refrigerant in the form of gas travels from the evaporators into a compressor, which is powered by an electric motor. The compressor squeezes the gas and pushes it through the fridge's pipes. As the gas is squeezed, it heats up.

4. A series of tubes called evaporators fills with the cold gas. The gas absorbs heat from everything in the fridge, which causes the fridge to chill down. The gas gets sucked into the compressor—and the cycle starts again.

Chillin'

Most freezers in home refrigerators go down to 0°F, which keeps ice cream nice and firm. But there are colder places than that. Check out the lowest of the low...temperatures.

○ On an average day, the temperature in the **Arctic** is about −30°F. The coldest temperature recorded in the Arctic is −89°F.

○ **Antarctica** is the world's coldest place, with winter temperatures reaching −94°F. Here, the coldest temperature ever on Earth was recorded: −135.8°F.

○ One of the coldest places in the universe is inside a **cosmic cloud.** These clouds of gas and dust are far from stars, and any radiation that reaches them is blocked by dust. The temperature inside one might be as cold as −425°F.

○ The coldest anything in the universe can get is −460°F. That's called **absolute zero.**

3. The liquid is pushed through a little hole called an expansion valve. When it passes through the hole, the liquid becomes a very cold gas.

FACTOID

Fred Wolf invented the first fridge that came with an ice tray built inside in 1913. The first metal ice tray that ejected ice cubes was invented in 1933 by Guy Tinkham.

HOW Can a Virus Make Your Computer Sick?

Just like people, computers can get sick from viruses. Computer viruses work like viruses that infect humans. They spread from computer to computer by making copies of themselves. Once inside a computer, a virus can do harm, such as making the computer run slowly or crash often, or by erasing the hard drive. Computer viruses are made and sent out by people who want to make trouble.

Computer viruses first began appearing in the 1980s. That's when the personal computer boom began. Computer users started downloading programs and exchanging floppy disks. That made the spread of viruses simple. Today, there are "cures" for computer viruses, and so virus creators must constantly find new ways to infect computers. So it's important for computer users to know the cause and symptoms of computer viruses.

Software virus: This is a small bit of software that gets into a computer and secretly attaches itself to other programs. Every time a user opens a program, the virus also opens and starts to run. It can reproduce itself by latching on to other programs. The virus program interferes with the workings of the computer, damages files, or causes annoying messages to appear on the screen. But it can't hurt hardware—the inner workings of the computer.

Trojan virus: In Greek mythology, soldiers hid inside a giant wooden horse. When the horse was brought into the city of Troy, the soldiers got out and attacked. In the same way, a Trojan virus will pretend to be a music, video, or some other program. But when the program is downloaded, the virus attacks the computer. These viruses can erase a hard drive, force the computer to show ads, or allow a hacker to gain partial control of your computer.

January 10, 2011 6:59:26 AM

1 Attachment, 3.5 MB   Save

E-mail virus: This type of virus is usually sent as an attachment. Some viruses will infect a computer even if the e-mail or preview panel are simply viewed. Once opened, the virus will mail itself to all the people in the e-mail address book. Those people in turn will often spread the virus to others, and so on.

Worm: This software program can copy itself from one computer to another without attaching itself to other programs. Worms can avoid security blocks and quickly spread from one computer to every computer in a network, including a company's or government organization's. Worms also spread through e-mail address books. Worms can destroy files and slow down or stop programs from working.

Safe Surfing

The Internet is a great tool, but it has its downsides. Protect yourself from becoming a cyber-victim by following these tips.

○ Talk with a parent about when and how you will use the Internet and send e-mails.

○ Never give out personal information online, such as your last name, home address, school, phone number, photos, where you hang out, or people you know without a parent's okay.

○ Don't share your password for your e-mail, social networking sites, or websites with anyone except your parent.

○ Never agree to meet someone in person you only met online without your parent's permission, and without a parent going with you to the meeting.

○ Get your parent's permission before signing up for a website.

○ Always discuss with your parent what websites you visit.

○ Don't be rude or a bully on the Internet. Treat everyone the way you want to be treated.

HOW Does Wi-Fi Connect to the Internet?

A hotspot sounds like a place to avoid. But not if you're a Wi-Fi user. Hotspots are areas where a computer can connect to the Internet without being plugged in to electrical, telephone, or cable lines. Wi-Fi, which stands for *wireless fidelity,* uses microwave signals to link computers to other computers or websites. Wi-Fi works almost anywhere. It lets a person go online while moving from room to room. Users can also connect to the Internet in a coffee shop, library, schoolroom, hotel, airport, or even in an airplane thousands of feet in the air. On a plane, the Wi-Fi signal is sent to a satellite, which beams it to Earth.

Almost all new laptops and many new desktop computers are set up for wireless use. If a computer doesn't come with wireless, a wireless adapter can be added to it. It may also need a special software program to connect to a wireless network.

To connect to the Internet, an **adapter** in the computer changes digital data into a radio signal. The radio signal is similar to those used to broadcast radio and TV shows. An antenna inside the computer transmits the radio signal to a device called a router.

A **router** is an electronic device that contains an antenna, which receives the signal sent by the computer. To work best, a router is placed near a computer and away from objects that might block its signal, such as walls or furniture. The router translates the information from the computer and sends it through a cable to a modem.

The modem links a computer to the Internet. It changes the digital information in the computer to a form that can be sent through phone or cable television lines. The signal goes to servers that change the signals back into a digital form. These servers are joined to form a network—the Internet. To receive Internet through Wi-Fi, the process works in reverse. A signal goes from the Internet to a modem to a router to a computer.

Going Wireless

The only thing that is possibly better than a wireless computer is a wireless video game. The GameCube for Nintendo in 2002 was the first popular console that had a wireless remote control. Four years later, Nintendo introduced the Wii. As players move the wireless controller, the figure on the screen moves as well. PlayStation Move for PS3 (shown here) is a wireless wand, or "controller." Its movements are tracked by a camera on the console.

In 2010, Microsoft introduced Kinect for Xbox 360. This is not only wireless—it drops the controller altogether. Kinect uses an infrared camera that instantly tracks the movements of the player's body and hands. When a player moves, the figure on the screen moves the same way. Who knows what the next wireless innovation will be?

For Wi-Fi to work properly, the computer should be no more than about 120 feet from the router. Outdoors, the maximum distance is around 300 to 500 feet. That allows people to use Wi-Fi outdoors in public spaces like a park, as well as in cafes and restaurants with hotspots.

HOW to Make Your Own Camera

The oldest and cheapest camera ever made is the camera obscura. Camera obscura means "dark chamber," which describes this simple device. A camera obscura is a dark room with a small hole in one wall. Light reflects off an object outside the wall. The light passes through the hole and makes an upside-down image of the object on the opposite wall. The image is very clear because a tiny hole focuses light. If the hole were large, the light hitting the wall would scatter and make the image of the object look blurry.

A camera obscura can only show what is directly outside the room. To view something else, you'd have to carry the room around. Since that isn't very practical, people made small, portable versions of the device, like the one in the photo above. And so can you.

What You Need

- An empty can shaped like a cylinder, with a metal bottom, such as a potato-chip can
- Wax paper or white tissue paper
- Thumbtack or pushpin
- Masking or electrical tape
- Ruler
- Marker
- Utility knife (ask an adult before using it)
- Aluminum foil

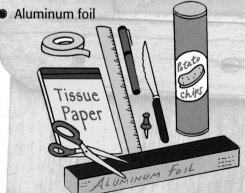

What to Do

1 With the ruler, measure two inches from the bottom of the can in two places and mark the spots. Connect the marks so the line goes around the can. Have an adult cut the can into two pieces along the line.

2 Use the thumbtack or pushpin to make a tiny hole in the center of the metal bottom of the can. Spin the tack in the hole to smooth the sides of the hole.

3 Cut out a circle of wax paper or tissue paper. Place it as tightly as possible over the open top of the short part of the can and tape it into place.

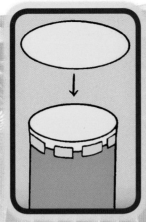

4 Place the long part of the can over the short part. Tape the two parts of the can together so it looks like it did before it was cut.

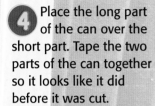

5 Wrap aluminum foil around the can, lining up the edges with the top and bottom of the can. If there is extra foil at the top, fold it into the can. Make sure no light enters the can except through the hole in the bottom and the opening at the top.

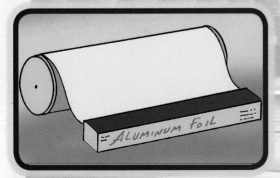

6 Place an object under bright light, point the pinhole at it, and view through the opening. Place your hands around the opening to keep out light. You should see the object on the wax paper, but upside down. Move your camera closer or farther away until the object is in focus.

Say Cheese!

Taking pictures with a digital camera is a snap. Still, to take good photos, it pays to explore what your camera can do.

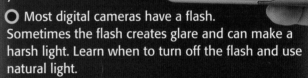

O Most digital cameras have a flash. Sometimes the flash creates glare and can make a harsh light. Learn when to turn off the flash and use natural light.

O A camera with a rotating lens lets you take pictures at different angles. You can even take a picture of yourself.

O If your camera comes with a burst mode, you can take several pictures in a row without waiting for the camera to recharge.

O When you shoot, try not to put the subject at the center of the photo.

O Use the horizontal lines in the view screen to make sure the picture is level.

O Don't be afraid to take a bad photo. After all, you can always delete it and try again.

Glossary

Antarctica the ice-covered continent around the South Pole
antenna a metal device used for sending and receiving radio waves
Arctic the area around the North Pole
avalanche a large mass of snow and ice that falls down the side of a mountain

bacteria microscopic single-celled organisms found in water, air, and soil
battery a device that produces an electrical current
burr the rough, prickly outside of a fruit

cells the basic structure of all living things; in a beehive, six-sided structures made of beeswax that store food and house growing bees
condensation the changing of gas into a liquid

decompose the process by which a dead organism rots away

e-waste electronic waste, such as computers or cell phones, that is thrown away
earthquake a trembling movement of Earth's crust that can damage buildings and other structures
electromagnetic field a magnetic field produced when electricity flows through a wire
electron a tiny particle that moves around the nucleus of an atom
endangered a species, or type of living thing, that is in immediate danger of becoming extinct, or dying out completely
evaporate to change a liquid into a gas, or vapor

fossil part of a plant or animal from the distant past that has been preserved in the Earth's crust
friction the force that one surface exerts on another when the two rub against each other

gear a wheel with teeth that turns another wheel with teeth, so the motion of one controls the speed of the other
generator a machine that changes mechanical energy into electrical energy, often by moving a copper wire through a magnetic field
greenhouse gas a gas, such as carbon dioxide and methane, that helps cause global warming

hurricane a storm that forms over tropical waters with winds that reach at least 74 miles per hour

infection the invasion of the body by a microorganism, such as a virus, that causes disease
infrared radiation electromagnetic waves that can't be seen by the human eye but can be sensed as heat
insulator a substance that doesn't allow heat or electricity to pass through it

kinetic energy the energy of movement

landfill a site designed so large amounts of trash can be buried safely

lightning a bright flash of light caused by electricity flowing from one part of a cloud to another or from a cloud to the surface of the Earth

magnetic field the lines of force created by and surrounding the sun and the planets

magnet an object that attracts or repels other magnets and attracts certain kinds of metal, such as iron and nickel

magnetosphere the magnetic field that surrounds a planet and which extends far into outer space

microwave electromagnetic radiation, similar to radio waves, that is used in microwave ovens to cook food

molecule the smallest part of a substance, made up of one or more atoms

pollution the contamination of air, water, or soil by harmful substances

potential energy stored energy

power surge a sudden, unexpected increase in electricity that can damage computers and other electrical equipment

radiation electromagnetic energy that moves in the form of waves

recycle to collect materials, such as metal cans and glass bottles, that have been thrown away in order to reuse them in new products

refrigerant a substance used in a refrigerator or air conditioner that lowers temperatures by absorbing heat

seed the part of a plant that can grow into a new plant

solar panel a device made up of solar cells, which change sunlight into electricity

static electricity electricity produced when two objects touch and separate

storm surge water that is pushed toward the shore by strong winds, often caused by hurricanes as they move near land

thermostat a device that controls the temperature in a room or an entire house

tornado a dark, funnel-shaped cloud made of fast-spinning air

ultraviolet radiation electromagnetic waves invisible to the human eye that can damage human cells

vapor a gas; also, tiny but visible particles that float in the air, such as smoke and steam

virus a tiny particle that can cause different types of illnesses by entering a person's body through the nose, mouth, or breaks in the skin

volt a measurement of how much force there is in an electric circuit

wind turbine a machine that turns the power of the wind into electrical energy

Credits

All illustrations and diagrams by Felipe Galindo unless indicated otherwise.

Cover: Mark Wainwright/Symbology Creative (background); Paul Orr/Shutterstock.com (flashlight); Iafoto/Shutterstock.com (tornado); Natykach Nataliia/Shutterstock.com (key); Jim Frazee/Moment/Getty Images (dog).

Back cover: Mark Wainwright/Symbology Creative (background); Vladislav Gurfinkel/Shutterstock.com (hurricane); Arcady/Shutterstock.com (sign); Potapov Alexander/Shutterstock.com (lightning); prudkov/Shutterstock.com (sky); Mark Wainwright/Symbology Creative (book covers); T-Design/Shutterstock.com (firefighter).

Interior: 1: Mark Wainwright/Symbology Creative (background); Courtesy of Dr. M. Eugene Rudd (camera); elina/Shutterstock.com (Earth); nodff/Shutterstock.com (single firefighter). 2–3: Zhana Ocheret/Shutterstock.com (background). 3: (dog); Elnur/Shutterstock.com (boy). 4–5: Kirschner/Shutterstock.com (background); vovan/Shutterstock.com (notebook paper). 5: Joe Zeff Design, Inc. for TIME For Kids (Earth). 6–7: Martin Fischer/Shutterstock.com (background); Robbi/Shutterstock.com (paper). 7: Fesus Robert/Shutterstock.com (lightning over water). 8–9: Njegovic/Shutterstock.com (background); jomphong/Shutterstock.com (paper). 9: arindambanerjee/Shutterstock.com (Haiti); Yai/Shutterstock.com (Concepción). 10–11: Mikadun/Shutterstock.com (background); Robbi/Shutterstock.com (paper). 10: AnetaPics/Shutterstock.com (dog). 11: nodff/Shutterstock.com (single firefighter); MISHELLA/Shutterstock.com (group of firefighters). 12–13: R. Gino Santa Maria/Shutterstock.com (background); nuttakit/Shutterstock.com (notebook); Iafoto/Shutterstock.com (tornado). 13: NOAA Photo Library, NOAA Central Library/OAR/ERL/National Severe Storms Laboratory (NSSL) (researcher); Minerva Studio/Shutterstock.com (diagram). 14–15: Tatagatta/Shutterstock.com (background); Andrea Booher/ FEMA News Photo (avalanche dog Mike Rieger/FEMA News Photo (disaster dog). 14: Marcella Miriello/Shutterstock.com (scent dog); Jim Parkin/Shutterstock.com (tracking dog). 15: Helping Hands: Monkey Helpers (capuchin monkey). 16–17: Febris/Shutterstock.com (background). 16: elina/Shutterstock.com (Earth). 17: Golden Pixels LLC/Shutterstock.com (hikers). 18–19: Lisa F. Young/Shutterstock.com (background); Lisa F. Young/Shutterstock.com (water and candles); Alhovik/Shutterstock.com (adhesive bandage). 18: David Valdez/FEMA (American Red Cross). 19: Christopher Elwell/Shutterstock.com (can opener); Mazzzur/Shutterstock.com (gloves); Gregory Gerber/Shutterstock.com (detergent); Lisa F. Young/Shutterstock.com (flashlights). 20–21: rezachka/Shutterstock.com (background). 20: BluIz60/Shutterstock.com (recycling plant); Marcel Paschertz/Shutterstock.com (copper). 21: imging/Shutterstock.com (stacking computers); 153203546/Shutterstock.com (disassembling); U.S. Environmental Protection Agency (circuits and wires). 22–23: Vera Volkova/Shutterstock.com (background). 22: U.S. Environmental Protection Agency (ENERGY STAR label). 24–25: majeczka/Shutterstock.com (background); TSpider/Shutterstock.com (turbine). 25: Atlaspix/Shutterstock.com (map). 26–27: rezachka/Shutterstock.com (background). 28–29: alexkar08/Shutterstock.com (background). 30–31: Natali Glado/Shutterstock.com (background). 31: Alexander Mak/Shutterstock.com (microwave); Courtesy of Raytheon (Percy Spencer); Courtesy of Raytheon (original microwave). 32–33: Adisa/Shutterstock.com (background). 33: Library of Congress Prints and Photographs Division (Harry Houdini). 34–35: Andrei Kuzmik/Shutterstock.com (background); megainarmy/Shutterstock.com (zipper). 35: Torsten Dietrich/Shutterstock.com (burdock plant); Keetten Predators/Shutterstock.com (shoes). 36–37: wonderisland/Shutterstock.com (background). 37: Volodymyr Goinyk/Shutterstock.com (Arctic); Gentoo Multimedia Limited/Shutterstock.com (penguins); NASA/JPL-Caltech/STScI (cosmic cloud). 38–39: bofotolux/Shutterstock.com (background); Axstokes/Shutterstock.com (computer screen). 38: Lightspring/Shutterstock.com (computer virus); Morphart Creation/Shutterstock.com (Trojan Horse). 39: Balefire/Shutterstock.com (computer worm); Zhana Ocheret/Shutterstock.com (sidebar background); Elnur/Shutterstock.com (boy). 40–41: Zhana Ocheret/Shutterstock.com (background). 40: valdis torms/Shutterstock.com (Wi-Fi icon); Greg da Silva/Shutterstock.com (boy); Norman Chan/Shutterstock.com (router). 41: Norman Chan/Shutterstock.com (modem); dboystudio/Shutterstock.com (park); Barone Firenze/Shutterstock.com (PlayStation Move). 42–43: Moreno Soppelsa/Shutterstock.com (background). 42: Courtesy of Dr. M. Eugene Rudd (camera obscura). 43: Murat Baysan/Shutterstock.com (digital camera). 44–45: Zhanna Ocheret/Shutterstock.com. 46: Guilu/Shutterstock.com. 47–48: Zhanna Ocheret/Shutterstock.com.

Index